# Reading

## Grade 3

## Table of Contents

- Reading comprehension
- Fact vs. opinion, fiction vs. non-fiction
- Reading resources and research skills
- Reading for pleasure and information
- And much more!

## Elaine J. Kenny, B.Ed.

## Syllables

To help you read a word you don't know, you can divide it into sections called **syllables**. Every **syllable** has a vowel. **Vowels** are **a e i o u**.

⇨ Example: pump · kin
Pumpkin has two **vowels** and two **syllables**.
Sound out **pump** and **kin** to make pumpkin.

Read the list of words and write each syllable you hear on the lines provided. The first one has been done for you.

| | 1st syllable | 2nd syllable | 3rd syllable | # of syllables |
|---|---|---|---|---|
| recess | re | cess | _____ | 2 |
| example | _____ | _____ | _____ | |
| because | _____ | _____ | _____ | |
| anything | _____ | _____ | _____ | |
| today | _____ | _____ | _____ | |
| summer | _____ | _____ | _____ | |
| excited | _____ | _____ | _____ | |
| together | _____ | _____ | _____ | |
| apple | _____ | _____ | _____ | |
| better | _____ | _____ | _____ | |
| another | _____ | _____ | _____ | |
| pioneers | _____ | _____ | _____ | |

## Compound Words

Sometimes two or more words are put together to make a new word called a **compound word**. To help read the new word, break it down into two smaller words and then read them together.

⇨ Example: sand + box = sandbox
  Sandbox is a **compound word**.

Read the list of words below. Draw a line between the words that make up the compound word. The first one is done for you.

sand | box        doghouse        breakfast

summertime        airplane        broomstick

dinnertime        timeline        campfire

nickname          pigpen          fingerprint

## More Compound Words

Read the compound words list.

| sailboats | sunburn | birthday | paintbrush | outdoors |
| barnyard | beehive | driveway | cardboard | sidewalk |

Read these sentences. Fill in the blanks with the compound word that fits best from the list. The first one has been done for you.

After being in the sun all day, I realized I had a ___sunburn___.

I always have a chocolate cake when it's my _____.

It's fun playing _____ in the summertime.

My dad parks his car in the _____.

Always clean your _____ with soap and water after you use it.

There are lots of _____ on the lake.

We get honey from a _____.

Remember to shovel the _____ in front of your house after it snows.

You can find cows and pigs in a _____.

Recycling _____ is a way to help our environment.

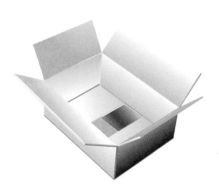

## Following Directions

Following directions is a very important skill. You use it to find a new place, follow a recipe, or complete a task.

Read the directions on how to make a super sundae. Read the ingredient choices listed. Draw and label your sundae on the following page based on the directions.

1. Choose two types of ice cream and put two scoops of each in the sundae dish.
2. Next, choose your favourite sauce to pour on top.
3. Choose two toppings to sprinkle over the sauce.
4. Add as much fruit as you like.
5. Finally, add one cherry on top.

**Ice Cream Flavours**
vanilla
chocolate
butterscotch
strawberry

**Sauces**
chocolate
caramel
strawberry
hot fudge

**Toppings**
nuts
marshmallows
sprinkles
chocolate chips

**Fruit**
pineapple chunks
sliced strawberries
sliced banana
blueberries
cherries

# Your Super Sundae!

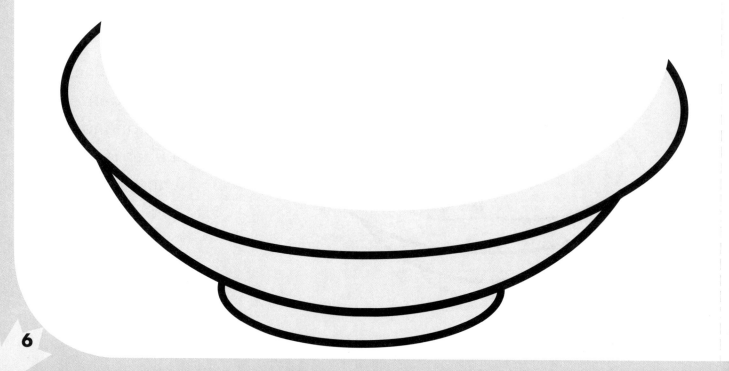

## Reading a Recipe

You must carefully follow directions when completing a recipe in order for it to turn out. Read the recipe for Simple Chocolate Brownies. Answer the questions on the following page.

### Simple Chocolate Brownies
#### Makes 12-24 Brownies

## Ingredients

1/2 cup (125 ml) butter
2 squares unsweetened chocolate
1 cup (250 ml) sugar
2 eggs, well beaten
1/2 teaspoon (2 ml) vanilla
3/4 cup (175 ml) flour
1/4 teaspoon (1 ml) salt
1/2 cup (125 ml) chopped walnuts (optional)

## Preparation

1. Preheat oven to 350° F
2. Melt butter and chocolate together over low heat.
   Remove from heat as soon as melted.
3. Slowly add beaten eggs stirring constantly.
4. Add remaining ingredients and stir.
5. Pour into a greased 8-inch (20 cm) square pan.
6. Bake for 25 to 30 minutes until a toothpick comes out clean.
7. Cool and cut into squares.

## Reading a Recipe

Answer these questions about the Simple Chocolate Brownies recipe on previous page. Write your answer in complete sentences.

How many squares of chocolate does the recipe need?

_____

_____

What needs to be well beaten before mixing with something else?

_____

_____

At what temperature is the oven set?

_____

_____

How long do the brownies take to bake?

_____

_____

What do you do last? (check one)

_____ Preheat the oven to 350° F.

_____ Cut the cooled brownies into squares.

_____ Pour into a greased 8-inch (20 cm) square pan.

What two ingredients do you measure in teaspoons?

_____

_____

How many brownies does the recipe make?

_____

## Sequencing

Sequencing means putting things in correct order. It is the order in which the events take place.

⇨ Example: I woke up, got out of bed, and went to the bathroom.

After brushing my teeth, I got dressed, ate breakfast, and left for school.

Read the sentences below about brushing your teeth. Number them in the correct order from 1 through 7 in the boxes.

Spit out the toothpaste. ☐

Put toothbrush and toothpaste away. ☐

Move brush around in your mouth. ☐

Wet the toothbrush and toothpaste with water. ☐

Get out your toothbrush and the toothpaste. ☐

Rinse off toothbrush. ☐

Squeeze toothpaste onto your toothbrush. ☐

## Sequencing

To understand the order in which things happen in a story, look for time order words like **first**, **next**, and **finally**.

Read the story. Answer the questions.

### The Campfire

Samantha helped her father start a campfire. First, she cleared the fire pit. Next, she set up lots of kindling that would burn quickly and then added two big logs that would burn more slowly. After striking the match and lighting the fire, she waited a few minutes to see if the wood had caught fire. Finally, Samantha put a hot dog on a long stick and held it just above the fire until it was cooked.

Answer the questions in complete sentences.

What did Samantha do first?

_____

_____

What did Samantha do last?

_____

_____

What was one other thing Samantha did to start the campfire?

_____

_____

## More Sequencing

Read the following sentences. Write them in the correct order on the lines provided.

### Carving a Pumpkin

Carve a face into the pumpkin.
Bring the pumpkin home.
Put a candle in the pumpkin.
Get out a sharp knife.
Cut off the top and scoop out the seeds.
Pick a pumpkin from the patch.
Light the candle and set outside when dark.

1. _____

2. _____

3. _____

4. _____

5. _____

6. _____

7. _____

## Compare and Contrast

If you **contrast** two things, you show how they are different. If you **compare** and **contrast** two things, you show how they are alike and how they are different.

Fill in the chart below to compare and contrast what it is like to live in Canada during the winter and during the summer.

### Canadian Winter and Summer

|  | Alike | Different |
|---|---|---|
| Weather |  |  |
| Activities |  |  |
| Food |  |  |
| Holidays |  |  |
| Clothing |  |  |

## Finding Hidden Meaning

At times, you may read something that has a phrase you need to interpret in order to understand the meaning.

⇨ Example: **She is as sweet as candy.**
   This sentence means she's a very nice girl.

Read the sentences. Circle a, b, or c for the sentence that best explains what the first sentence means.

⇨ Example: One bad apple spoils the whole bushel.
   a. The apples are in a bunch.
   (b.) One bad person can have a bad effect on everyone around him or her.
   c. Apples spoil.

Kill two birds with one stone.
   a. You kill birds with stones.
   b. Complete two tasks with one action.
   c. Birds are dying.

Don't judge a book by its cover!
   a. Don't read books with covers you don't like.
   b. You must look inside the book to judge it.
   c. You shouldn't judge a person by his or her looks alone.

Everyone is in the same boat.
   a. Everyone is sailing together.
   b. Everyone is facing the same problem.
   c. The boat is big enough to carry many people.

## Main Idea

The **main idea** is the most important meaning of something you read. It does not include less important details.

Read these passages. Answer the questions.

Ken is very active. He gets up early every morning and goes for a jog before school. Ken rides his bike to school instead of taking the bus.

What is the main idea?
a. Ken likes school.
b. Ken is fit.
c. Ken likes to ride his bike.

Lisa developed a business plan. She decided to walk dogs for people in the neighbourhood. Lisa created posters and went door to door looking for customers. Lisa got so many customers that she had to hire her friend Elaine to help.

What is the main idea?
a. Lisa is friendly.
b. Lisa likes dogs.
c. Lisa worked hard to make her plan work.

## Main Idea

Remember that the **main idea** is the basic meaning of the reading material. It is the most important message in the writing.

Read the paragraph. Answer the questions.

Almost everyone likes to eat pizza. In fact, pizza is eaten all over the world. Many different toppings can be put on pizza. The most popular one in Canada is pepperoni. Pizza has ingredients from all four food groups. The crust is a grain product, the cheese is a milk product, the tomato sauce is a vegetable, and the pepperoni is meat. It can be a very healthy dinner if you add a salad on the side and a cold glass of milk.

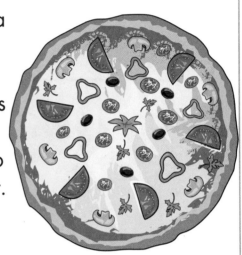

What is the main idea of the paragraph? Answer in a complete sentence.

_____

_____

_____

_____

Which of the following statements is **not true**? Circle a, b, c, or d.
- a. Pizza is a healthy dinner.
- b. Pizza is only sold in Canada.
- c. Pizza has ingredients from all four food groups.
- d. There are many different toppings that can be put on pizza.

## Making Predictions

A good reader uses information in a text and what he or she already knows to think about what might happen next.

Read each sentence beginning. Circle the best sentence ending. The first one has been done for you.

If you eat too much candy before going to bed, your stomach is likely to feel

    a. great
    (b. sick)
    c. empty

If you put water on a slice of bread, it is likely to get

    a. soggy
    b. bigger
    c. hard

If a dog bites you, you are likely to feel

    a. happy
    b. angry
    c. curious

If you leave a popsicle on the counter on a summer day, it is likely to

    a. stay the same
    b. harden
    c. melt

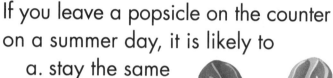

If you put your hand on a burning log, it is likely to

    a. hurt
    b. tickle
    c. feel great

If you work hard on an assignment, you are likely to

    a. fail
    b. get a good mark
    c. not learn anything

## Making Predictions

Read each passage. Circle a, b, or c for the sentence that best answers each question.

### Big Brother

Damian walks his little brother to school every day. Damian holds his hand and helps him safely cross the street. One day, Damian forgot his backpack at home. He had a math assignment in it that he needed for class. Damian always does his best at school.

Which sentence tells what will most likely happen next?

a. Damian will leave his brother alone and go home to get his backpack.
b. Damian will walk back home taking his little brother safely with him.
c. Damian will continue walking to school and not hand in his assignment.

### The Zoo

Mazari went to the zoo with her father. It was a great day! She loved seeing all the animals and spending time outdoors with her dad. When Mazari got home, she told her mom about all the things she had seen at the zoo.

Which sentence tells what will likely happen next?

a. Mazari will forget all about her day.
b. Mazari will read all about different zoos.
c. Mazari's father will forbid her from going to the zoo again.

## Making Predictions

Read the passage. Answer the question.

### Basketball

Roshawn has never made a school team before. He used to be one of the shortest boys in his class, but this year he has grown so much that now he is the tallest. Every Saturday morning, Roshawn plays basketball at the community centre. He has learned how to dribble and shoot very well.

What do you think will happen when Roshawn tries out for the basketball team? Make a prediction.

_____

_____

Study the pictures. Answer the questions.

What do you think is going to happen to the flower? Make a prediction.

_____

_____

_____

_____

Why do you think so? _____

## Facts and Opinions

A **fact** is something that is real and true. An **opinion** is a statement reflecting the writer's beliefs.

⇨ Examples: **Facts**

> There are 7 days in a week.
> The Canadian flag is red and white.

**Opinions**

Pizza is better than broccoli.
The Canadian flag is the most beautiful flag in the world.

Read each sentence. Put an **F** in the box if the sentence is a **fact**. Put an **O** in the box if the sentence is an **opinion**. The first one is done for you.

Boys are always taller than girls. **O**

July comes after June in the calendar year. ☐

Ottawa is in Canada. ☐

Dogs are smarter than cats. ☐

July 1st is Canada Day. ☐

Summer is everyone's favourite time of year. ☐

Eating an apple a day will keep the doctor away. ☐

If you find a penny and pick it up you will have good luck. ☐

Smoking is bad for your health. ☐

There is a maple leaf on Canada's flag. ☐

Maple syrup comes from maple trees. ☐

Drinking milk can make your bones stronger. ☐

## Sorting Facts and Opinions

Good readers sort out information as they read. They decide if the information is a fact or an opinion.

### Fact

When you don't know if something is a fact, you can look for proof that it is true. For example, if someone says it is two o'clock, you can check a clock to be sure. Sometimes, you need to look up a fact. Some of the sources you might use include Wikipedia, almanacs, textbooks, biographies, and encyclopedias. Facts answer the questions who, what, when, where, why, and how.

### Opinion

An opinion is what the writer thinks or believes. It is the author's judgment on a certain topic. Opinions are found in many kinds of writing. They sometimes can be mistaken for facts. The editorial page of a newspaper is set aside for opinions. People can have different opinions based on the same set of facts.

Look at the pictures. Read each sentence. Write an **F** if the sentence is a **fact**. Write an **O** if the sentence is an **opinion**.

Canada

Japan

There are five flags. _____
The Canadian flag is the most beautiful. _____
The Irish flag is orange, green, and white. _____
The Japanese flag is easy to identify. _____
The United States of America's flag is red, white, and blue. _____
The Canadian flag is the most unique. _____
The flag of Sudan has the most colours. _____

Ireland

USA

Write another fact about the pictures.

Sudan

_____

Write another opinion about the pictures.

_____

## Sorting Facts and Opinions

A piece of writing often includes both facts and opinions.
Read the paragraph. Answer the questions.

> Lacrosse is Canada's national summer sport. First Nations people, who were the first people to live in what is now Canada, invented lacrosse many years ago as part of a ceremony. Later, other people who came to settle in Canada started to play the game too. Lacrosse can be played inside an arena or outside on a field. You will like to play lacrosse if you like to play hockey. You use a lacrosse stick and a hard rubber ball. Lacrosse is the best game ever!

Write "fact" or "opinion" next to each sentence.

Lacrosse is Canada's national summer sport. _____

Lacrosse is the best game ever! _____

First Nations people invented lacrosse many years ago. _____

You will like lacrosse if you like hockey. _____

Write another fact from the paragraph.

_____

_____

_____

_____

_____

## Context Clues

Context clues are words in a sentence or surrounding sentences that help you understand a word you don't know.

⇨ Example: The dinosaur bones in the museum are **enormous**. They take up almost all the space in the room.

If you don't know what **enormous** means, you can figure it out from the next sentence: take up all the space in the room.

Underline the words that help you figure out the meaning of the green word or phrase. Answer the questions.

⇨ Example: The drive-in movie began after **dusk**, just after the sunset. What is the meaning of dusk?

   Dusk is when it is starting to get dark.

Paul is a **meteorologist**, a person who studies weather patterns. What is a meteorologist?

_____

After adding **fertilizer**, the plants in my garden grew quickly. They produced large, beautiful flowers. What is fertilizer?

_____

She said she could run a marathon without getting thirsty, but I felt **dubious** about it. What does dubious mean?

_____

After school, I'm always **ravenous**. I can't seem to get enough to eat to fill me up! What does ravenous mean?

_____

The twins show signs of **telepathy**. They can communicate with each other without speaking a word. What does telepathy mean?

_____

## Fiction and Non-Fiction

**Non-fiction** books contain facts. They might tell about a real person like Terry Fox, or about real animals, places, or events.

**Fiction** books contain made up stories that come from the writer's imagination. They could be about aliens or talking animals or anything the writer thinks of. Some books include a mixture of some real events or people from the past and some make-believe events and characters. This is called historical fiction.

Look at the list of book titles below. Put them in either the fiction column or the non-fiction column.

*Cinderella*
*Building the Canadian National Railway*
*Father Bear Bakes a Cake*
*How to Build a Birdhouse*
*The City Mouse and the Country Mouse*
*The Life of Alexander Graham Bell*
*Tom and Jerry Adventures*
*Canada's Lakes and Rivers*

| Fiction | Non-fiction |
|---|---|
| _____ | _____ |
| _____ | _____ |
| _____ | _____ |
| _____ | _____ |
| _____ | _____ |

## A Non-Fiction Story

Read the story. Answer the questions on the next page.

### The School Trip

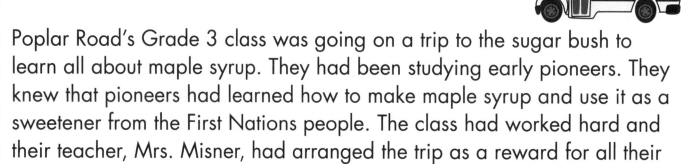

Poplar Road's Grade 3 class was going on a trip to the sugar bush to learn all about maple syrup. They had been studying early pioneers. They knew that pioneers had learned how to make maple syrup and use it as a sweetener from the First Nations people. The class had worked hard and their teacher, Mrs. Misner, had arranged the trip as a reward for all their hard work.

The bus pulled in front of the school and the students all boarded. They were off! After about 30 minutes, the bus pulled into a Conservation Area. It was beautiful! A guide named Susan met them as the students all filed out of the bus. She led the students along a path towards the sugar shack, pointing out the sap buckets along the way. Soon the group arrived at an area that had a beautiful fire going and a large black pot hanging over it. Susan explained to the students that the sap they had seen being collected along the way was boiling in the pot over the fire. She explained the steps needed to turn the sap into syrup.

Susan told the students to take a seat on the logs around the fire. Next, she went into the sugar shack and came out with plates piled high with pancakes for each student. Mrs. Misner was given a jug of maple syrup to pour over the pancakes. The students loved the treat and all agreed that Canadian maple syrup was one of the best things that the early pioneers learned to make from the First Nations people. It was a great day!

## A Non-Fiction Story

After reading the non-fiction story, "The School Trip," answer these questions. Write the main events in the order they happened in the story.

1._____

_____

2._____

_____

3._____

_____

4._____

_____

5._____

_____

Draw each event in the order that they happened in the story.

## A Fictional Story

Read the story. Answer the questions on the next page.

### Summer Camp

Jeffrey was nervous. In less than one week he was leaving to go to camp for the first time. Jeffrey had read about camp and his older brother Sam had gone for the last two summers, but he still couldn't help being scared. Jeffrey was always scared when he tried new things.

On Saturday morning, his mom and dad woke him at 8 o'clock so he could have a good breakfast before leaving for camp. Jeffrey's stomach flipped as he saw his bags beside the front door. He calmed himself down during breakfast by pretending he wasn't leaving, but that didn't last long. Before he knew it the car was packed and the family was on their way.

As they drove, Jeffrey's family told him funny stories about when they had been at camp. Sam talked about a time when he fell out of a canoe and got soaked. Jeffrey's mom talked about meeting lots of friends and the funny pranks they played on each other.

When they arrived at camp, Jeffrey met his counsellor and the rest of the boys in his cabin. He said a tearful goodbye to his family and then set up his sleeping bag and gear. That night Jeffrey found it really hard to get to sleep. All he could think about was his family.

The next morning finally came. After breakfast it was time for a canoe lesson. Jeff found out he liked something called "gunwale bobbing" and that the other boys in his cabin were really nice. Before he knew it, the day was over and it was time to go to sleep. The rest of the week flew by. Jeffrey tried many new things. He went canoeing and kayaking. He went hiking in the woods with a map and compass. Jeffrey even slept outdoors on the last night!

Jeffrey was sad when he woke up on the last morning. He couldn't believe how much fun camp had been. When his mom and dad arrived, Jeffrey gave them both a big hug and said he was counting down the days until next summer when he would be going to camp again!

## A Fictional Story

Answer these questions about the fictional story, "Summer Camp". Write your answers in complete sentences.

Why was Jeffrey so nervous?

_____

_____

_____

What were some of the things his family did to help Jeffrey feel better?

_____

_____

_____

Was there a time when you were nervous about something?

_____

_____

_____

What did Jeffrey learn about himself while he was at camp?

_____

_____

_____

# Reading Comprehension

## Setting

The **setting** of a story is when and where it takes place. It describes the time and different places in a story.

Read each description and circle the correct time and place.

| Description | Time | Place |
|---|---|---|
| As I opened my eyes, I saw the bright sunlight shining on my bed. I quickly jumped up and scurried around to get dressed as fast as I could. | evening<br><br>afternoon<br><br>morning | school<br><br>home<br><br>hockey arena |
| Even though it was dark, I knew where we were. My mom was carrying the popcorn and I was carrying the drinks. We sat down and anxiously waited for it to start. | morning<br><br>afternoon<br><br>evening | gym<br><br>movie theatre<br><br>dentist |
| The mid-day sun shone into my eyes as I tried to catch my friends. I climbed up the slide, hoping to tag someone at the top. | morning<br><br>afternoon<br><br>evening | garage<br><br>playground<br><br>store |

| Description | Time | Place |
|---|---|---|
| "Please, can't I stay up and watch the hockey game," I begged. "Sorry," said Mom. "Tomorrow you have a really early game yourself so you need your sleep." | morning<br><br>afternoon<br><br>evening | store<br><br>school<br><br>home |
| "Your assignment is due tomorrow, first thing in the morning. Please put up your chairs as you leave. See you tomorrow," said my teacher. | morning<br><br>afternoon<br><br>evening | playground<br><br>school<br><br>home |
| The stars were out as I ran up the driveway. I wanted to get to the T.V. before my brother so I could pick the show we were going to watch. | morning<br><br>afternoon<br><br>evening | museum<br><br>school<br><br>home |

### Fiction

Read the story. Answer the questions on the next page.

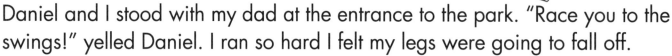

## A Trip to the Park
by Ahsan Rahim-Zada

Daniel and I stood with my dad at the entrance to the park. "Race you to the swings!" yelled Daniel. I ran so hard I felt my legs were going to fall off.

"Hey Dad, can you come and push us, pretty please?" My dad came over and pushed both of us at once! I went so high I felt like I could reach up and grab a piece of the clouds and bring it down. When we jumped off, I felt a little dizzy. "Let's go down the slide now," I said to Daniel.

"Mr. Morra, could you please push us down the slide?" asked Daniel. Then we went down zippy fast to the bottom. "Let's go on the monkey bars now," Daniel said.

Uh, oh, I thought. You see, the thing is Daniel is in Grade 4 and I am in Grade 3 and the monkey bars wobble. My dad says they are at least five feet high so you have to jump to get on them.

"Hurry up, Matthew!" yelled Daniel. So I walked slowly over, thinking, I can do this! Daniel had already done it so he was waiting on the other side. I jumped up and, yes, I grabbed the first bar! Only 9 more.

"Just think one hand, two hand," said Daniel.

"Okay, so one and two, one and two, one and two, one and two, one and two, one and two, one and two, one and two, one and two!"

"Matthew, you did it!" yelled Daniel.

"Way to go, Sport!" said my dad.

"Wow, I did it."

"Okay, guys, time to go," my dad said.

"Hey, Dad? Can we come back tomorrow?"

"Sure thing Matthew, and Daniel can come too."

So that was my most favourite trip to the park.

## Fiction

After reading "A Trip to the Park," answer these questions.
Write your answers in complete sentences.

Why was Matthew so nervous?

_____

_____

_____

Why did Matthew start counting to himself?

_____

_____

_____

Have you ever felt this way before trying something new? What did you do?

_____

_____

_____

Do you think that having Daniel there helped Matthew complete the monkey bars? Why or why not?

_____

_____

_____

## Setting

Draw the setting for "A Trip to the Park".

## Non-Fiction Article

Read the article. Answer the questions about the article on the next page.

### Canadian Pioneer Life

Canada was settled in the late 1700's and early 1800's by people from many parts of the world. These settlers were called pioneers.

Pioneers came to Canada for different reasons. Some came to start a new life in a country where there were many opportunities to better themselves. Others came to own land of their own. Many of the countries they had come from were crowded and had little food. Canada offered a new home with lots of space and food for everyone.

The pioneers came from many different countries. Pioneers travelled by boat from England, Scotland, Ireland, Italy, Germany, and France. Other pioneers lived in what is now the United States of America. These pioneers travelled north by land to Canada.

When the pioneers arrived in Canada they faced many hardships. Most of them had no experience with Canada's long and cold winters so their first winter here was really tough.

The First Nations people in the area were very helpful and taught the pioneers many survival skills to help them through the winter. In Canada, the pioneers were given free land, an axe, and some seed to plant crops. They had to clear the land and build their own homes with the logs they had cut. All their tools and utensils were made from the resources on their land. They either grew their own food, or found it in the forest. Life was hard. However, for most pioneers it was much better than the life they had left.

## Non-Fiction Article

After reading the non-fiction article "Canadian Pioneer Life," answer these questions. Write your answers in complete sentences.

List three reasons why the early pioneers came to Canada.

1._____

_____

2._____

_____

3._____

List three places the early pioneers left to come to Canada.

1._____

2._____

3._____

Describe what the pioneers had to do when they came to Canada.

_____

_____

_____

_____

## Parts of a Book

A book is made up of different parts. Learning the parts of a book will help you become a better reader.

### Book Cover

A book cover is the first thing you see when reading a book. Often the title will give you a hint about what the book is about. If there is a picture too, it helps you predict what the book might be about. The book cover includes the title of the book and the author's name.

⇨ Example:

**Book Title**
Picture helps predict what the book is about.

**Author's Name**

**Prediction:** This book is probably about a trip to a far away place that includes a plane ride.

THE BIG TRIP

By
Amanda Anderson

Read the book cover. Predict what the book is about.

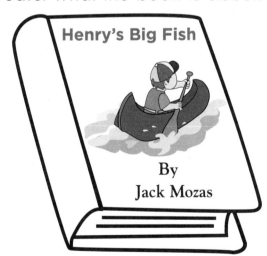

Henry's Big Fish

By
Jack Mozas

Title: _____

Author: _____

Prediction: _____

## Book Cover

Read the book covers. Predict what the book is about.

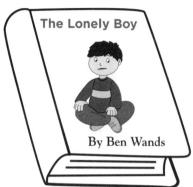

Title: _____

Author: _____

Prediction: _____

Title: _____

Author: _____

Prediction: _____

Title: _____

Author: _____

Prediction: _____

## Book Cover

Design a book cover of your own!

What do you think a reader might predict about the book from your cover?

_____

_____

## Book Cover

Draw a line to match each cover to its pages. Underline the books that could be non-fiction (true stories). Circle the books that could be fiction (make-believe stories).

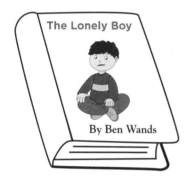

## Table of Contents

The **table of contents** lists the titles of the chapters in the book and the page that each chapter starts on. In a non-fiction book, the chapter titles tell you what information you will find in each chapter.

**Early Settlers**
*Table of Contents*

Use the table of contents above to answer these questions.

What is the name of the chapter that begins on page 23?

_____

If you want to learn more about the First Nations, where would you look?

_____

Where would you look to find out why the settlers came to Canada?

_____

Where would you learn about what the early settlers ate?

_____

## Glossary

A **glossary** is usually found at the back of a book. It lists specific words from the book and tells what those words mean. It is like a dictionary made just for that book. Read the glossary below. Answer the questions.

conifers (con·i·fers) — trees or bushes that have waxy, needle-like or scaly leaves; most of these trees are evergreens.

deciduous (de·cid·u·ous) — trees that shed their leaves in the fall

legume (le·gume) — dry fruit with seeds attached to its inner wall; an example is a pea pod

nectar (nec·tar) — a sweet, sticky substance produced by plants to attract insects

Answer these questions in complete sentences.

What type of tree loses its leaves in the fall?

_____

What is a legume?

_____

What are two types of trees?

_____

How many syllables in the word deciduous?

_____

What attracts insects?

_____

## Parts of a Book

### Index

An **index** is found at the back of a book. It lists the topics in the book and the pages where you will find information about those topics in the book. Indexes are found mostly in non-fiction books. The index is always in alphabetical order. Read the index below. Answer the questions.

*Index*

| | |
|---|---|
| Arrows | 5, 6, 7, 8 |
| Bones | 19, 20 |
| Dwellings | 39, 40, 54, 55, 56 |
| Food | 9, 10, 11, 12 |
| Hunting Techniques | 26, 27, 28, 29, 30 |
| Nomadic People | 41, 42, 43 |
| Totem Poles | 23, 24, 25 |
| Wigwams | 39 |

Answer these questions in complete sentences.

On what pages would you look to find out more about totem poles?

_____

What topic in the book starts on page 26?

_____

What do you learn about on page 9?

_____

What two things can you find on page 39?

_____

Where would you look to find out about hunting techniques?

_____

## Review – Parts of the Book Match-Up

Draw a line from Column A to the correct definition in Column B.

| Column A | Column B |
|---|---|
| glossary | tells the title and author of the book |
| book cover | tells about what the chapter is all about |
| table of contents | lists words used in the book and their meanings |
| chapter heading | shows where to look up information on a topic in the book |
| index | lists the chapters and the pages they start on |

## Dictionary, Encyclopedia, and Atlas

### Resources

The material you read to help you learn about, research, and understand a topic are called reading resources. Dictionaries, encyclopedias, and atlases are examples of resources. These resources are available as books and on the internet.

### Dictionary

A dictionary contains lots and lots of words. A dictionary is used to learn how to say words, spell words, and understand what words mean. The words in a dictionary are always in alphabetical order.

### Encyclopedia

An encyclopedia has lots of information about many different topics in it. An encyclopedia is a good place to start when researching people, places, and things. It could be a book or an on-line resource such as Wikipedia.

### Atlas

An atlas is packed with information about specific places like countries or cities and geographical features such as mountains, rivers, and oceans. An atlas contains lots of maps, charts, and graphs to help you. It is a good resource when you need to answer geography questions.

## Research Skills

Read the following sentences. Write what resource you would use to answer the questions: dictionary, encyclopedia, or atlas?

⇨ Example: Where is Ireland? _____**Atlas**_____

How do cars accelerate? _____

What does the word "knight" mean? _____

Where is the Atlantic Ocean? _____

Why do hummingbirds flap their wings so quickly? _____

How many syllables are in the word "geography"? _____

Who was Terry Fox and what did he do? _____

Which country is south of Canada? _____

Did Canada fight in Word War I? _____

What does the word "apothecary" mean? _____

Is "a-n-t" the correct way to spell the word that refers to a small insect?

_____

Where is Victoria? _____

## Autobiographies

An **autobiography** is a book that tells the
true story of a person's life. It is always written
by the person who is the topic of the book.
Answer the questions about yourself in complete
sentences.

Where were you born?

_____

_____

Who are the members of your family?

_____

What activities do you like to do?

_____

What is your favourite subject in school? Why is it your favourite?

_____

What is your favourite television show? Why is it your favourite?

_____

How many pets have you had? What kind of pet would
you like to have now?

_____

If you could do anything when you grow up, what would you like to do?

_____

## Biographies

A **biography** is a book that tells the true story of a person's life. It is always written by a person who is not the topic of the book. It can be about someone who is alive now or someone who was alive a long time ago.
Examples of some biographies:

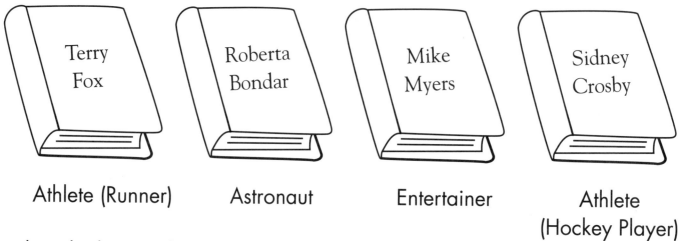

| Terry Fox | Roberta Bondar | Mike Myers | Sidney Crosby |
| Athlete (Runner) | Astronaut | Entertainer | Athlete (Hockey Player) |

Look at the biography examples. Answer these questions.
In which **biography** would you read about:

A person who has travelled in space?

_____

A person who has starred in movies?

_____

A person who spends lots of time on the ice?

_____

A person who likes to keep moving?

_____

Which biography would you like to read? Why?

_____

## Reading a Letter

A **letter** is a form of communication between people.

*August 29, 20XX*

*Dear Grandma,*
*I'm writing to let you know how my summer has been. It has been so long since I've seen you and I really miss our talks.*
*In July, I spent two weeks at camp. I had a great time swimming and canoeing. I met lots of new friends. August was spent at the cottage where I learned to play chess. It is a great game! I love sleeping in and having lots of free time to do fun things.*
*School is nearly here. I'm not looking forward to getting up early every day or having homework to do at night. I hope to see you soon.*

*Lots of love,*
*Brad*

Read the letter.
Answer each question with yes or no.

Did Brad like camp? _____

Is Brad looking forward to school? _____

Did Brad learn to play chess? _____

Could Brad sleep in at the cottage? _____

Does Brad like to go canoeing? _____

Has Brad seen his Grandma lately? _____

## Write a Letter

Write your own letter to a friend describing your last special family day.

## Posters

A **poster** is used to display information in words and pictures. It uses both words and pictures so the reader can understand the full meaning of the poster. Often important information is written in larger letters so that the reader can easily see it.

**FOUND CAT**
She was found at
11 Alberta Place on
Saturday, October 22

She has an orange coat with small
patches of white on her belly.
Her eyes are blue and her tail is bent.

She is really friendly.

If she is yours please call:
Elaine at 416-555-1234

Read the poster. Circle the correct answer or answer the questions in complete sentences.

The cat is        white          orange          grey

She has a bent      whisker          ear          tail

She was found on       October 22       January 9       September 16

How can you reach the person who made the poster?

_____

Is the cat friendly?

_____

## Design a Poster

Design a poster about something you want to sell.
Remember to include both words and pictures.
Remember to include a way for the reader to reach you.

## Advertisements and Flyers

An advertisement or flyer is used by stores to display the things they sell and the price. It is important to be able to read them in order to save money where possible.

### CLAIRE'S CANDY STORE

**Lollipops**
Sale: 5 for $1.00
Regular: 50¢ each

**Licorice**
Sale: 99¢ for 250 g pack
Regular: $1.98 for 250 g pack

**Chocolate Bars**
Sale: 2 for $1.00
Regular: 89¢ each

**Jawbreakers**
Sale: 4 for $1.00
Regular: 50¢ each

**Gummy Bears**
Sale: $2.99 for 454 g pack
Regular: $3.99 for 454 g pack

**Jube Jubes**
Sale: $1.99 for 454 g pack
Regular: $3.49 for 454 g pack

**Sale on until September 5, 20XX**

### Advertisements and Flyers

Read the advertisement/flyer on the previous page.
Circle **true** or **false** after each sentence.

| | | |
|---|---|---|
| The jube jubes cost $1.99. | true | false |
| The lollipops used to be 50¢ each. | true | false |
| The licorice is the least expensive candy. | true | false |
| Chocolate bars are 89¢ on sale. | true | false |
| Jawbreakers are 3 for a dollar. | true | false |
| Gummy bears are less expensive than jube jubes. | true | false |

Answer these questions in complete sentences.

What is your favourite kind of candy? Why is it your favourite?

_____

_____

_____

Eating candy too much is not good for you. Why?

_____

_____

_____

## Great Books for Kids

These are some books that are recommended by kids to read alone or with a grown-up. Ask a grown-up to go to the library with you, pick one out, and get reading! Tell a friend about the books you like!

*Alligator Pie* by Dennis Lee
*Anne of Green Gables* by Lucy Maud Montgomery
*The Cremation of Sam McGee* by Robert W. Service
*Emma's Magic Winter* by Jean Little
*The Hockey Sweater* by Roch Carrier
*The Incredible Journey* by Sheila Burnford
*Owls in the Family* by Farley Mowat
*The Trumpet of the Swan* by E.B. White
*Burp! The Most Interesting Book You'll Ever Read About Eating*
  by Diane Swanson
*The Boxcar Children* by Gertrude Chandler Warner
  (This one has over a hundred books in the series!)

## Book Log

Keep track of the books you read and what you like.
Write the title and author on the line and then add your comments.

Title and Author:

_____

_____

Circle your thoughts:     I loved it!     It was good     Just okay     Not for me

Title and Author:

_____

_____

Circle your thoughts:     I loved it!     It was good     Just okay     Not for me

Title and Author:

_____

_____

Circle your thoughts:     I loved it!     It was good     Just okay     Not for me

Title and Author:

_____

_____

Circle your thoughts:     I loved it!     It was good     Just okay     Not for me

Title and Author:

_____

_____

Circle your thoughts:      I loved it!      It was good      Just okay      Not for me

Title and Author:

_____

_____

Circle your thoughts:      I loved it!      It was good      Just okay      Not for me

Title and Author:

_____

_____

Circle your thoughts:      I loved it!      It was good      Just okay      Not for me

Title and Author:

_____

_____

Circle your thoughts:      I loved it!      It was good      Just okay      Not for me

Title and Author:

_____

_____

Circle your thoughts:      I loved it!      It was good      Just okay      Not for me

## Page 2

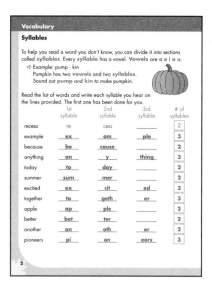

### Vocabulary

**Syllables**

To help you read a word you don't know, you can divide it into sections called syllables. Every syllable has a vowel. Vowels are a e i o u.

↪ Example: pump · kin
Pumpkin has two vowels and two syllables.
Sound out pump and kin to make pumpkin.

Read the list of words and write each syllable you hear on the lines provided. The first one has been done for you.

| | 1st syllable | 2nd syllable | 3rd syllable | # of syllables |
|---|---|---|---|---|
| recess | re | cess | | 2 |
| example | ex | am | ple | 3 |
| because | be | cause | | 2 |
| anything | an | y | thing | 3 |
| today | to | day | | 2 |
| summer | sum | mer | | 2 |
| excited | ex | cit | ed | 3 |
| together | to | geth | er | 3 |
| apple | ap | ple | | 2 |
| better | bet | ter | | 2 |
| another | an | oth | er | 3 |
| pioneers | pi | on | eers | 3 |

## Page 3

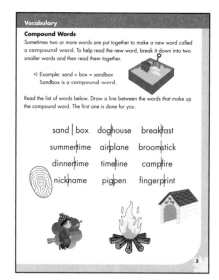

### Vocabulary

**Compound Words**

Sometimes two or more words are put together to make a new word called a compound word. To help read the new word, break it down into two smaller words and then read them together.

↪ Example: sand + box = sandbox
Sandbox is a compound word.

Read the list of words below. Draw a line between the words that make up the compound word. The first one is done for you.

sand | box    dog|house    break|fast
summer|time    air|plane    broom|stick
dinner|time    time|line    camp|fire
nick|name    pig|pen    finger|print

## Page 4

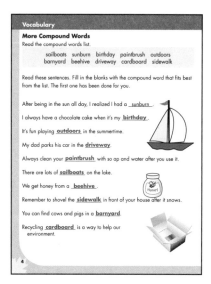

### Vocabulary

**More Compound Words**

Read the compound words list.

sailboats  sunburn  birthday  paintbrush  outdoors
barnyard  beehive  driveway  cardboard  sidewalk

Read these sentences. Fill in the blanks with the compound word that fits best from the list. The first one has been done for you.

After being in the sun all day, I realized I had a __sunburn__.

I always have a chocolate cake when it's my __birthday__.

It's fun playing __outdoors__ in the summertime.

My dad parks his car in the __driveway__.

Always clean your __paintbrush__ with soap and water after you use it.

There are lots of __sailboats__ on the lake.

We get honey from a __beehive__.

Remember to shovel the __sidewalk__ in front of your house after it snows.

You can find cows and pigs in a __barnyard__.

Recycling __cardboard__ is a way to help our environment.

## Page 7

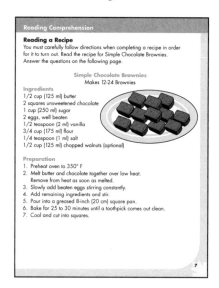

### Reading Comprehension

**Reading a Recipe**

You must carefully follow directions when completing a recipe in order for it to turn out. Read the recipe for Simple Chocolate Brownies. Answer the questions on the following page.

**Simple Chocolate Brownies**
Makes 12-24 Brownies

**Ingredients**
1/2 cup (125 ml) butter
2 squares unsweetened chocolate
1 cup (250 ml) sugar
2 eggs, well beaten
1/2 teaspoon (2 ml) vanilla
3/4 cup (175 ml) flour
1/4 teaspoon (1 ml) salt
1/2 cup (125 ml) chopped walnuts (optional)

**Preparation**
1. Preheat oven to 350° F.
2. Melt butter and chocolate together over low heat. Remove from heat as soon as melted.
3. Slowly add beaten eggs stirring constantly.
4. Add remaining ingredients and stir.
5. Pour into a greased 8-inch (20 cm) square pan.
6. Bake for 25 to 30 minutes until a toothpick comes out clean.
7. Cool and cut into squares.

## Page 8

### Reading Comprehension

**Reading a Recipe**

Answer these questions about the Simple Chocolate Brownies recipe on previous page. Write your answer in complete sentences.

How many squares of chocolate does the recipe need?
__The recipe needs two squares of chocolate.__

What needs to be well beaten before mixing with something else?
__The eggs need to be well beaten.__

At what temperature is the oven set?
__The oven is set at 350 degrees F.__

How long do the brownies take to bake?
__The brownies should bake for 25 to 30 minutes.__

What do you do last? (check one)
☐ Preheat the oven to 350° F.
☑ Cut the cooled brownies into squares.
☐ Pour into a greased 8-inch (20 cm) square pan.

What two ingredients do you measure in teaspoons?
__You measure vanilla and salt in teaspoons.__

How many brownies does the recipe make?
__The recipe makes 12 to 24 brownies.__

## Page 9

### Reading Comprehension

**Sequencing**

Sequencing means putting things in correct order. It is the order in which the events take place.

↪ Example: I woke up, got out of bed, and went to the bathroom. After brushing my teeth, I got dressed, ate breakfast, and left for school.

Read the sentences below about brushing your teeth. Number them in the correct order from 1 through 7 in the boxes.

Spit out the toothpaste.  5
Put toothbrush and toothpaste away.  7
Move brush around in your mouth.  4
Wet the toothbrush and toothpaste with water.  3
Get out your toothbrush and the toothpaste.  1
Rinse off toothbrush.  6
Squeeze toothpaste onto your toothbrush.  2

## Page 10

**Reading Comprehension**

### Sequencing

To understand the order in which things happen in a story, look for time order words like **first**, **next**, and **finally**.

Read the story. Answer the questions.

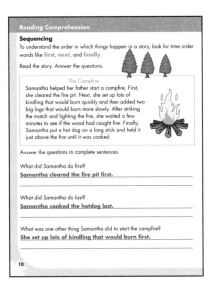

**The Campfire**

Samantha helped her father start a campfire. First, she cleared the fire pit. Next, she set up lots of kindling that would burn quickly and then added two big logs that would burn more slowly. After striking the match and lighting the fire, she waited a few minutes to see if the wood had caught fire. Finally, Samantha put a hot dog on a long stick and held it just above the fire until it was cooked.

Answer the questions in complete sentences.

What did Samantha do first?
**Samantha cleared the fire pit first.**

What did Samantha do last?
**Samantha cooked the hotdog last.**

What was one other thing Samantha did to start the campfire?
**She set up lots of kindling that would burn first.**

## Page 11

**Reading Comprehension**

### More Sequencing

Read the following sentences. Write them in the correct order on the lines provided.

**Carving a Pumpkin**
Carve a face into the pumpkin.
Bring the pumpkin home.
Put a candle in the pumpkin.
Get out a sharp knife.
Cut off the top and scoop out the seeds.
Pick a pumpkin from the patch.
Light the candle and set outside when dark.

1. **Pick a pumpkin from the patch.**
2. **Bring the pumpkin home.**
3. **Get out a sharp knife.**
4. **Cut off the top and scoop out the seeds.**
5. **Carve a face into the pumpkin.**
6. **Put a candle in the pumpkin.**
7. **Light the candle and set outside when dark.**

## Page 12

**Reading Comprehension**

### Compare and Contrast

If you **contrast** two things, you show how they are different. If you **compare** and **contrast** two things, you show how they are alike and how they are different.

Fill in the chart below to compare and contrast what it is like to live in Canada during the winter and during the summer.

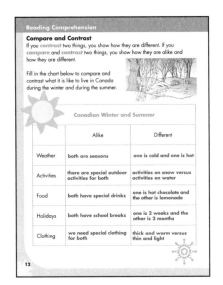

**Canadian Winter and Summer**

|  | Alike | Different |
|---|---|---|
| Weather | both are seasons | one is cold and one is hot |
| Activities | there are special outdoor activities for both | activities on snow versus activities on water |
| Food | both have special drinks | one is hot chocolate and the other is lemonade |
| Holidays | both have school breaks | one is 2 weeks and the other is 2 months |
| Clothing | we need special clothing for both | thick and warm versus thin and light |

## Page 13

**Reading Comprehension**

### Finding Hidden Meaning

At times, you may read something that has a phrase you need to interpret in order to understand the meaning.

◇ Example: **She is as sweet as candy.**
This sentence means she's a very nice girl.

Read the sentences. Circle a, b, or c for the sentence that best explains what the first sentence means.

◇ Example: One bad apple spoils the whole bushel.
  a. The apples are in a bunch.
  b. One bad person can have a bad effect on everyone around him or her.
  c. Apples spoil.

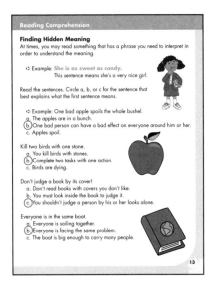

Kill two birds with one stone.
  a. You kill birds with stones.
  b. Complete two tasks with one action.
  c. Birds are dying.

Don't judge a book by its cover!
  a. Don't read books with covers you don't like.
  b. You must look inside the book to judge it.
  c. You shouldn't judge a person by his or her looks alone.

Everyone is in the same boat.
  a. Everyone is sailing together.
  b. Everyone is facing the same problem.
  c. The boat is big enough to carry many people.

## Page 14

**Reading Comprehension**

### Main Idea

The **main idea** is the most important meaning of something you read. It does not include less important details.

Read these passages. Answer the questions.

Ken is very active. He gets up early every morning and goes for a jog before school. Ken rides his bike to school instead of taking the bus.

What is the main idea?
  a. Ken likes school.
  b. Ken is fit.
  c. Ken likes to ride his bike.

Lisa developed a business plan. She decided to walk dogs for people in the neighbourhood. Lisa created posters and went door to door looking for customers. Lisa got so many customers that she had to hire her friend Elaine to help.

What is the main idea?
  a. Lisa is friendly.
  b. Lisa likes dogs.
  c. Lisa worked hard to make her plan work.

## Page 15

**Reading Comprehension**

### Main Idea

Remember that the **main idea** is the basic meaning of the reading material. It is the most important message in the writing.

Read the paragraph. Answer the questions.

Almost everyone likes to eat pizza. In fact, pizza is eaten all over the world. Many different toppings can be put on pizza. The most popular one in Canada is pepperoni. Pizza has ingredients from all four food groups. The crust is a grain product, the cheese is a milk product, the tomato sauce is a vegetable, and the pepperoni is meat. It can be a very healthy dinner if you add on a salad on the side and a cold glass of milk.

What is the main idea of the paragraph? Answer in a complete sentence.

**The main idea is that pizza is a popular and healthy food.**

Which of the following statements is **not true**? Circle a, b, c, or d.
  a. Pizza is a healthy dinner.
  b. Pizza is only sold in Canada.
  c. Pizza has ingredients from all four food groups.
  d. There are many different toppings that can be put on pizza.

# Solutions

## Page 16

**Making Predictions**
A good reader uses information in a text and what he or she already knows to think about what might happen next.

Read each sentence beginning. Circle the best sentence ending. The first one has been done for you.

If you eat too much candy before going to bed, your stomach is likely to feel
a. great
**b. sick** (circled)
c. empty

If you put water on a slice of bread, it is likely to get
**a. soggy** (circled)
b. bigger
c. hard

If a dog bites you, you are likely to feel
a. happy
**b. angry** (circled)
c. curious

If you leave a popsicle on the counter on a summer day, it is likely to
a. stay the same
b. harden
**c. melt** (circled)

If you put your hand on a burning log, it is likely to
**a. hurt** (circled)
b. tickle
c. feel great

If you work hard on an assignment, you are likely to
a. fail
**b. get a good mark** (circled)
c. not learn anything

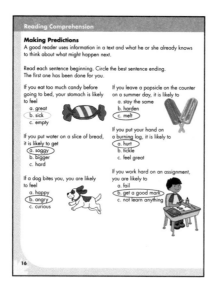

## Page 17

**Making Predictions**
Read each passage. Circle a, b, or c for the sentence that best answers each question.

**Big Brother**
Damian walks his little brother to school every day. Damian holds his hand and helps him safely cross the street. One day, Damian forgot his backpack at home. He had a math assignment in it that he needed for class. Damian always does his best at school.

Which sentence tells what will most likely happen next?

a. Damian will leave his brother alone and go home to get his backpack.
**b. Damian will walk back home taking his little brother safely with him.** (circled)
c. Damian will continue walking to school and not hand in his assignment.

**The Zoo**
Mazari went to the zoo with her father. It was a great day! She loved seeing all the animals and spending time outdoors with her dad. When Mazari got home, she told her mom about all the things she had seen at the zoo.

Which sentence tells what will likely happen next?

a. Mazari will forget all about her day.
**b. Mazari will read all about different zoos.** (circled)
c. Mazari's father will forbid her from going to the zoo again.

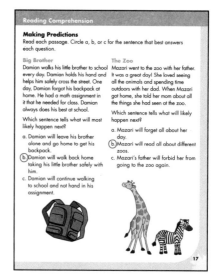

## Page 18

**Making Predictions**
Read the passage. Answer the question.

**Basketball**
Roshawn has never made a school team before. He used to be one of the shortest boys in his class, but this year he has grown so much that now he is the tallest. Every Saturday morning, Roshawn plays basketball at the community centre. He has learned how to dribble and shoot very well.

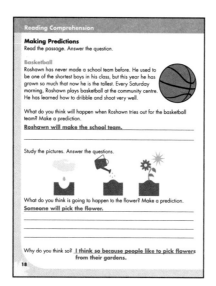

What do you think will happen when Roshawn tries out for the basketball team? Make a prediction.
**Roshawn will make the school team.**

Study the pictures. Answer the questions.

What do you think is going to happen to the flower? Make a prediction.
**Someone will pick the flower.**

Why do you think so? **I think so because people like to pick flowers from their gardens.**

## Page 19

**Facts and Opinions**
A fact is something that is real and true. An opinion is a statement reflecting the writer's beliefs.

Examples: **Facts**
There are 7 days in a week.
The Canadian flag is red and white.
**Opinions**
Pizza is better than broccoli.
The Canadian flag is the most beautiful flag in the world.

Read each sentence. Put an F in the box if the sentence is a fact. Put an O in the box if the sentence is an opinion. The first one is done for you.

Boys are always taller than girls. **O**
July comes after June in the calendar year. **F**
Ottawa is in Canada. **F**
Dogs are smarter than cats. **O**
July 1st is Canada Day. **F**
Summer is everyone's favourite time of year. **O**
Eating an apple a day will keep the doctor away. **O**
If you find a penny and pick it up you will have good luck. **O**
Smoking is bad for your health. **F**
There is a maple leaf on Canada's flag. **F**
Maple syrup comes from maple trees. **F**
Drinking milk can make your bones stronger. **F**

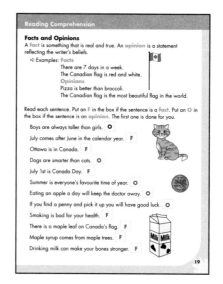

## Page 20

**Sorting Facts and Opinions**
Good readers sort out information as they read. They decide if the information is a fact or an opinion.

**Fact**
When you don't know if something is a fact, you can look for proof that it is true. For example, if someone says it is two o'clock, you can check a clock to be sure. Sometimes, you need to look up a fact. Some of the sources you might use include Wikipedia, almanacs, textbooks, biographies, and encyclopedias. Facts answer the questions who, what, when, where, why, and how.

**Opinion**
An opinion is what the writer thinks or believes. It is the author's judgment on a certain topic. Opinions are found in many kinds of writing. They sometimes can be mistaken for facts. The editorial page of a newspaper is set aside for opinions. People can have different opinions based on the same set of facts.

Look at the pictures. Read each sentence. Write an F if the sentence is a fact. Write an O if the sentence is an opinion.

There are five flags. **F**
The Canadian flag is the most beautiful. **O**
The Irish flag is orange, green, and white. **F**
The Japanese flag is easy to identify. **O**
The United States of America's flag is red, white, and blue. **F**
The Canadian flag is the most unique. **O**
The flag of Sudan has the most colours. **F**

Canada
Japan
Ireland
USA
Sudan

Write another fact about the pictures.
**Another fact is that the flags all have some white on them.**

Write another opinion about the pictures.
**Red is the best colour to have on a flag.**

## Page 21

**Sorting Facts and Opinions**
A piece of writing often includes both facts and opinions. Read the paragraph. Answer the questions.

Lacrosse is Canada's national summer sport. First Nations people, who were the first people to live in what is now Canada, invented lacrosse many years ago as part of a ceremony. Later, other people who came to settle in Canada started to play the game too. Lacrosse can be played inside an arena or outside on a field. You will like to play lacrosse if you like to play hockey. You use a lacrosse stick and a hard rubber ball. Lacrosse is the best game ever!

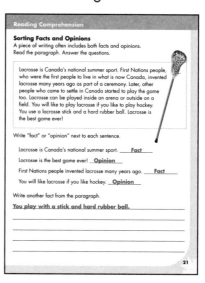

Write "fact" or "opinion" next to each sentence.

Lacrosse is Canada's national summer sport. **Fact**
Lacrosse is the best game ever! **Opinion**
First Nations people invented lacrosse many years ago. **Fact**
You will like lacrosse if you like hockey. **Opinion**

Write another fact from the paragraph.
**You play with a stick and hard rubber ball.**

## Page 22

**Reading Comprehension**

**Context Clues**

Context clues are words in a sentence or surrounding sentences that help you understand a word you don't know.

⇨ Example: The dinosaur bones in the museum are enormous. They take up almost all the space in the room.

If you don't know what **enormous** means, you can figure it out from the next sentence: take up all the space in the room.

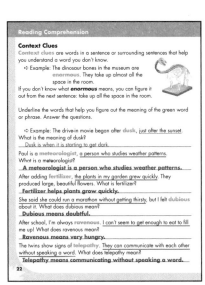

Underline the words that help you figure out the meaning of the green word or phrase. Answer the questions.

⇨ Example: The drive-in movie began after dusk, just after the sunset.
What is the meaning of dusk?
__Dusk is when it is starting to get dark.__

Paul is a meteorologist, a person who studies weather patterns.
What is a meteorologist?
__A meteorologist is a person who studies weather patterns.__

After adding fertilizer, the plants in my garden grew quickly. They produced large, beautiful flowers. What is fertilizer?
__Fertilizer helps plants grow quickly.__

She said she could run a marathon without getting thirsty, but I felt dubious about it. What does dubious mean?
__Dubious means doubtful.__

After school, I'm always ravenous. I can't seem to get enough to eat to fill me up! What does ravenous mean?
__Ravenous means very hungry.__

The twins show signs of telepathy. They can communicate with each other without speaking a word. What does telepathy mean?
__Telepathy means communicating without speaking a word.__

22

**Page 22**

## Page 23

**Reading Comprehension**

**Fiction and Non-Fiction**

Non-fiction books contain facts. They might tell about a real person like Terry Fox, or about real animals, places, or events.

Fiction books contain made up stories that come from the writer's imagination. They could be about aliens or talking animals or anything the writer thinks of. Some books include a mixture of some real events or people from the past and some make-believe events and characters. This is called historical fiction.

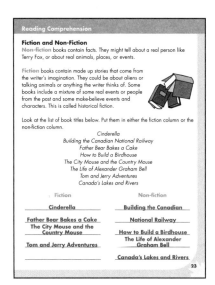

Look at the list of book titles below. Put them in either the fiction column or the non-fiction column.

*Cinderella*
*Building the Canadian National Railway*
*Father Bear Bakes a Cake*
*How to Build a Birdhouse*
*The City Mouse and the Country Mouse*
*The Life of Alexander Graham Bell*
*Tom and Jerry Adventures*
*Canada's Lakes and Rivers*

| Fiction | Non-fiction |
|---|---|
| **Cinderella** | **Building the Canadian** |
| **Father Bear Bakes a Cake** | **National Railway** |
| **The City Mouse and the Country Mouse** | **How to Build a Birdhouse** |
| **Tom and Jerry Adventures** | **The Life of Alexander Graham Bell** |
| | **Canada's Lakes and Rivers** |

23

**Page 23**

## Page 24

**Reading Comprehension**

**A Non-Fiction Story**

Read the story. Answer the questions on the next page.

**The School Trip**

Poplar Road's Grade 3 class was going on a trip to the sugar bush to learn all about maple syrup. They had been studying early pioneers. They knew that pioneers had learned how to make maple syrup and use it as a sweetener from the First Nations people. The class had worked hard and their teacher, Mrs. Misner, had arranged the trip as a reward for all their hard work.

The bus pulled in front of the school and the students all boarded. They were off! After about 30 minutes, the bus pulled into a Conservation Area. It was beautiful! A guide named Susan met them as the students all filed out of the bus. She led the students along a path towards the sugar shack, pointing out the sap buckets along the way. Soon the group arrived at an area that had a beautiful fire going and a large black pot hanging over it. Susan explained to the students that the sap they had seen being collected along the way was boiling in the pot over the fire. She explained the steps needed to turn the sap into syrup.

Susan told the students to take a seat on the logs around the fire. Next, she went into the sugar shack and came out with plates piled high with pancakes for each student. Mrs. Misner was given a jug of maple syrup to pour over the pancakes. The students loved the treat and all agreed that Canadian maple syrup was one of the best things that the early pioneers learned to make from the First Nations people. It was a great day!

24

**Page 24**

## Page 25

**Reading Comprehension**

**A Non-Fiction Story**

After reading the non-fiction story, "The School Trip," answer these questions. Write the main events in the order they happened in the story.

1. __The class was going on a trip as a reward for hard work.__

2. __A guide named Susan met them when they arrived at the Conservation Area.__

3. __Susan showed them how maple syrup was made by pioneers.__

4. __Susan gave each student pancakes.__

5. __Mrs. Misner gave everyone syrup to put on their pancakes.__

Draw each event in the order that they happened in the story.

25

**Page 25**

## Page 27

**Reading Comprehension**

**A Fictional Story**

Answer these questions about the fictional story, "Summer Camp". Write your answers in complete sentences.

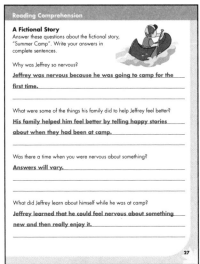

Why was Jeffrey so nervous?
__Jeffrey was nervous because he was going to camp for the first time.__

What were some of the things his family did to help Jeffrey feel better?
__His family helped him feel better by telling happy stories about when they had been at camp.__

Was there a time when you were nervous about something?
__Answers will vary.__

What did Jeffrey learn about himself while he was at camp?
__Jeffrey learned that he could feel nervous about something new and then really enjoy it.__

27

**Page 27**

## Page 28

**Reading Comprehension**

**Setting**

The setting of a story is when and where it takes place. It describes the time and different places in a story.

Read each description and circle the correct time and place.

| Description | Time | Place |
|---|---|---|
| As I opened my eyes, I saw the bright sunlight shining on my bed. I quickly jumped up and scurried around to get dressed as fast as I could. | evening / afternoon / (morning) | school / (home) / hockey arena |
| Even though it was dark, I knew where we were. My mom was carrying the popcorn and I was carrying the drinks. We sat down and anxiously waited for it to start. | morning / afternoon / (evening) | gym / (movie theatre) / dentist |
| The mid-day sun shone into my eyes and I tried to catch my friends. I climbed up the slide, hoping to tag someone at the top. | morning / (afternoon) / evening | garage / (playground) / store |

28

**Page 28**

# Solutions

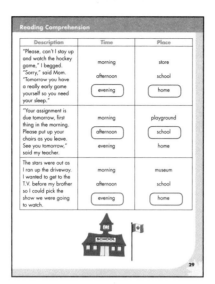

**Reading Comprehension**

| Description | Time | Place |
|---|---|---|
| "Please, can't I stay up and watch the hockey game," I begged. "Sorry," said Mom. "Tomorrow you have a really early game yourself so you need your sleep." | morning / afternoon / (evening) | store / school / (home) |
| "Your assignment is due tomorrow, first thing in the morning. Please put up your chairs as you leave. See you tomorrow," said my teacher. | morning / (afternoon) / evening | playground / (school) / home |
| The stars were out as I ran up the driveway. I wanted to get to the T.V. before my brother so I could pick the show we were going to watch. | morning / afternoon / (evening) | museum / school / (home) |

**Page 29**

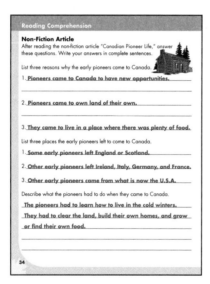

**Reading Comprehension**

**Non-Fiction Article**
After reading the non-fiction article "Canadian Pioneer Life," answer these questions. Write your answers in complete sentences.

List three reasons why the early pioneers came to Canada.

1. Pioneers came to Canada to have new opportunities.

2. Pioneers came to own land of their own.

3. They came to live in a place where there was plenty of food.

List three places the early pioneers left to come to Canada.

1. Some early pioneers left England or Scotland.

2. Other early pioneers left Ireland, Italy, Germany, and France.

3. Other early pioneers came from what is now the U.S.A.

Describe what the pioneers had to do when they came to Canada.

The pioneers had to learn how to live in the cold winters. They had to clear the land, build their own homes, and grow or find their own food.

**Page 34**

**Reading Comprehension**

**Fiction**
After reading "A Trip to the Park," answer these questions. Write your answers in complete sentences.

Why was Matthew so nervous?

Matthew was nervous because the monkey bars were up high and they wobbled.

Why did Matthew start counting to himself?

Counting helped him think about what he needed to do to succeed.

Have you ever felt this way before trying something new? What did you do?

Answers will vary.

Do you think that having Daniel there helped Matthew complete the monkey bars? Why or why not?

Yes, Daniel helped Matthew by encouraging him. Matthew might not have tried the monkey bars if Daniel had not been there.

**Page 31**

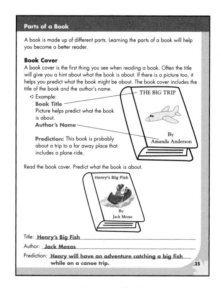

**Parts of a Book**

A book is made up of different parts. Learning the parts of a book will help you become a better reader.

**Book Cover**
A book cover is the first thing you see when reading a book. Often the title will give you a hint about what the book is about. If there is a picture too, it helps you predict what the book might be about. The book cover includes the title of the book and the author's name.

Example:

**Book Title**
Picture helps predict what the book is about.

**Author's Name**

THE BIG TRIP
By Amanda Anderson

**Prediction:** This book is probably about a trip to a far away place that includes a plane ride.

Read the book cover. Predict what the book is about.

Henry's Big Fish
By Jack Mozas

Title: Henry's Big Fish

Author: Jack Mozas

Prediction: Henry will have an adventure catching a big fish while on a canoe trip.

**Page 35**

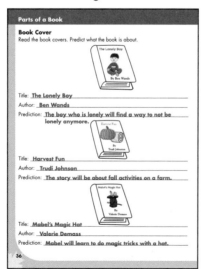

**Parts of a Book**

**Book Cover**
Read the book covers. Predict what the book is about.

The Lonely Boy
By Ben Wands

Title: The Lonely Boy

Author: Ben Wands

Prediction: The boy who is lonely will find a way to not be lonely anymore.

Harvest Fun
By Trudi Johnson

Title: Harvest Fun

Author: Trudi Johnson

Prediction: The story will be about fall activities on a farm.

Mabel's Magic Hat
By Valerie Demass

Title: Mabel's Magic Hat

Author: Valerie Demass

Prediction: Mabel will learn to do magic tricks with a hat.

**Page 36**

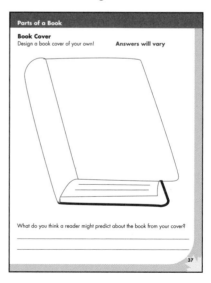

**Parts of a Book**

**Book Cover**
Design a book cover of your own!       Answers will vary

What do you think a reader might predict about the book from your cover?

**Page 37**

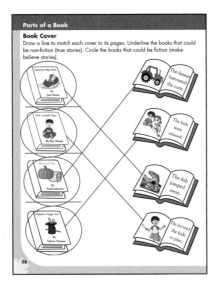

Page 38

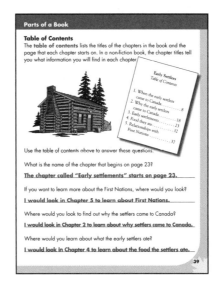

Page 39

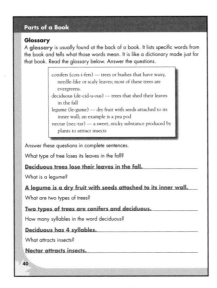

Page 40

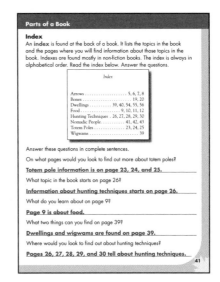

Page 41

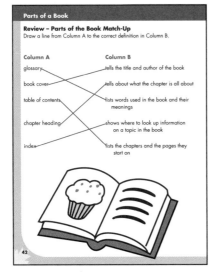

Page 42

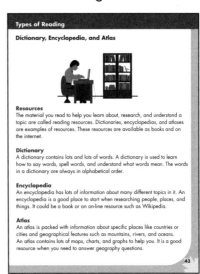

Page 43

## Page 44

**Types of Reading**

**Research Skills**
Read the following sentences. Write what resource you would use to answer the questions: dictionary, encyclopedia, or atlas?

Example: Where is Ireland? __Atlas__

How do cars accelerate? __Encyclopedia__

What does the word "knight" mean? __Dictionary__

Where is the Atlantic Ocean? __Atlas__

Why do hummingbirds flap their wings so quickly? __Encyclopedia__

How many syllables are in the word "geography"? __Dictionary__

Who was Terry Fox and what did he do? __Encyclopedia__

Which country is south of Canada? __Atlas__

Did Canada fight in Word War I? __Encyclopedia__

What does the word "apothecary" mean? __Dictionary__

Is "a-n-t" the correct way to spell the word that refers to a small insect?
__Dictionary__

Where is Victoria? __Atlas__

## Page 45

**Types of Reading**

**Autobiographies**
An **autobiography** is a book that tells the true story of a person's life. It is always written by the person who is the topic of the book. Answer the questions about yourself in complete sentences.

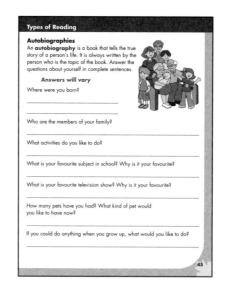

**Answers will vary**

Where were you born?

Who are the members of your family?

What activities do you like to do?

What is your favourite subject in school? Why is it your favourite?

What is your favourite television show? Why is it your favourite?

How many pets have you had? What kind of pet would you like to have now?

If you could do anything when you grow up, what would you like to do?

## Page 46

**Types of Reading**

**Biographies**
A **biography** is a book that tells the true story of a person's life. It is always written by a person who is not the topic of the book. It can be about someone who is alive now or someone who was alive a long time ago.
Examples of some biographies:

| Terry Fox | Roberta Bondar | Mike Myers | Sidney Crosby |
|---|---|---|---|
| Athlete (Runner) | Astronaut | Entertainer | Athlete (Hockey Player) |

Look at the biography examples. Answer these questions.
In which **biography** would you read about:
A person who has travelled in space?
__Roberta Bondar__

A person who has starred in movies?
__Mike Myers__

A person who spends lots of time on the ice?
__Sidney Crosby__

A person who likes to keep moving?
__Terry Fox__

Which biography would you like to read? Why?
__Answers will vary.__

## Page 47

**Types of Reading**

**Reading a Letter**
A **letter** is a form of communication between people.

> *August 29, 20XX*
>
> *Dear Grandma,*
> *I'm writing to let you know how my summer has been. It has been so long since I've seen you and I really miss our talks.*
> *In July, I spent two weeks at camp. I had a great time swimming and canoeing. I met lots of new friends. August was spent at the cottage where I learned to play chess. It is a great game! I love sleeping in and having* Answers will vary *ots of free time to do fun things.*
> *School is nearly here. I'm not looking forward to getting up early every day or having homework to do at night. I hope to see you soon.*
>
> *Lots of love,*
> *Brad*

Read the letter.
Answer each question with yes or no.

Did Brad like camp? __yes__
Is Brad looking forward to school? __no__
Did Brad learn to play chess? __yes__
Could Brad sleep in at the cottage? __yes__
Does Brad like to go canoeing? __yes__
Has Brad seen his Grandma lately? __no__

## Page 48

**Types of Reading**

**Write a Letter**
Write your own letter to a friend describing your last special family day.

Answers will vary.

## Page 49

**Types of Reading**

**Posters**
A **poster** is used to display information in words and pictures. It uses both words and pictures so the reader can understand the full meaning of the poster. Often important information is written in larger letters so that the reader can easily see it.

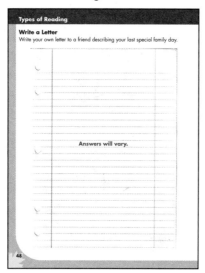

> **FOUND CAT**
> She was found at
> 11 Alberta Place on
> Saturday, October 22
>
> She has an orange coat with small patches of white on her belly. Her eyes are blue and her tail is bent.
>
> She is really friendly.
>
> If she is yours please call:
> Elaine at 416-555-1234

Read the poster. Circle the correct answer or answer the questions in complete sentences.
The cat is white (orange) grey
She has a bent whisker ear (tail)
She was found on (October 22) January 9 September 16
How can you reach the person who made the poster?
__Telephone the person who found the cat.__
Is the cat friendly?
__Yes__

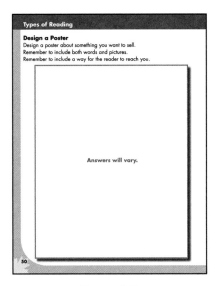

Page 50

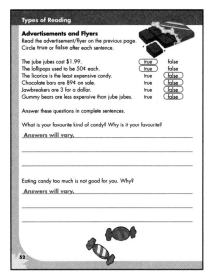

Page 52

# Good job!